CONGRESS

A TRUE BOOK

by
Patricia Ryon Quiri

Children's Press®
A Division of Grolier Publishing

New York London Hong Kong Sydney
Danbury, Connecticut

Reading Consultant
Linda Cornwell
Learning Resource Consultant
Indiana Department
of Education

For Ruth Muir,
my Grand Rapids mom.
With love

The Capitol at night,
Washington, D.C.

Visit Children's Press on the Internet at:
http://publishing.grolier.com

Library of Congress Cataloging-in-Publication Data

Quiri, Patricia Ryon.
   Congress / by Patricia Ryon Quiri.
      p.   cm. — (A true book)
   Includes bibliographical references and index.
   Summary: Describes the origins, functions, and duties of the United
States Congress. Includes an explanation of how to write a letter to a
member of Congress.
   ISBN 0-516-20662-1 (lib.bdg.)   0-516-26428-1 (pbk.)
   1. United States. Congress—Juvenile literature. [1. United States.
Congress.] I. Title. II. Series.
   JK1025Q57 1998   97-50484
                                            CIP
                                            AC

Contents

Holding a white flag, the British surrender to Washington, ending the Revolutionary War.

The Birth of a Free America

In 1776, the United States declared its independence from Britain. Americans wanted to have their own government. They were tired of Britain telling them what to do. They knew they would have to fight long and hard to become independent. The

Declaration of Independence signaled the beginning of the American Revolutionary War.

In 1883, the war came to an end. The United States had become an independent nation. Now it faced another difficult task. The country needed a stronger central government. It needed laws and principles to keep its states working together.

The Constitutional Convention

In May 1787, fifty-five Americans came to the State House in Philadelphia to draw up the plans for a federal government. They called their meeting the Constitutional Convention. Over a period of four months, the members of

The Constitutional Convention in Philadelphia brought together the finest leaders in the country.

the Constitutional Convention made a plan that would please all the states. There were arguments about the basic principles and details of this plan. Some of the delegates even threatened to walk out of the meeting. But eventually, a plan for government was written up. That plan became known as the U.S. Constitution.

The Constitution provided for three branches of federal government. These branches were to be the executive, the judicial, and the legislative. The executive branch would be headed by a president,

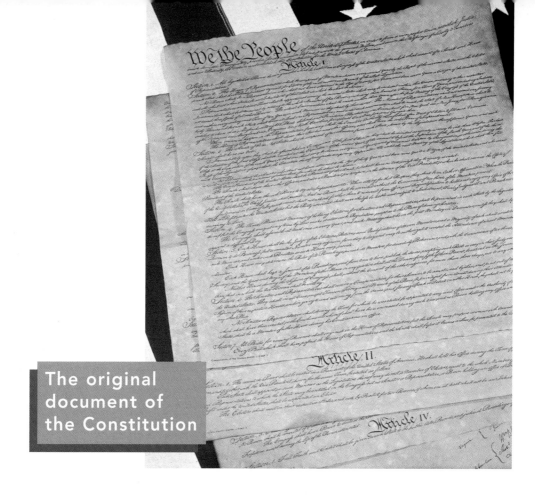

who would see that the laws of
the country were obeyed. The
judicial branch would see that
the laws of the country were
understood, and the legislative

branch—the Congress—would make the laws.

Two parts, or houses, would make up the Congress—the House of Representatives and the Senate. The members of the House of Representatives and the Senate would be chosen by the people. The number of members from each state would be based on the number of people living in that state. States with larger populations would have more members than states with smaller populations.

Smaller states, like New Jersey, didn't like this plan. They felt it would give the larger states more control in the government. William Paterson of New Jersey came up with another plan. It became known as the New Jersey Plan. Paterson's plan gave each state the same number of representatives. He didn't want population considered.

The Great Compromise

Two men from Connecticut, Roger Sherman and Oliver Ellsworth, came up with another solution. They suggested that in one house of Congress—the House of Representatives—the number of members from each state should be based on that state's population. The other

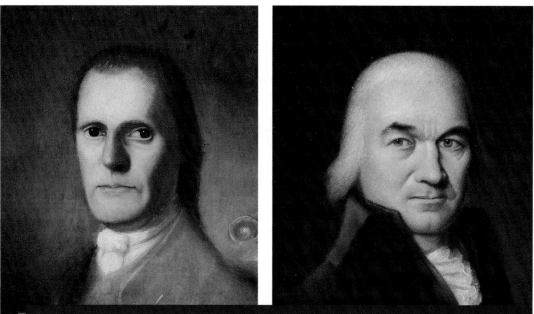
Roger Sherman (left) and Oliver Ellsworth (right), who proposed the Great Compromise

house—the Senate—would have two members from each state. This solution was accepted, because it pleased both the large states and the small states. The plan

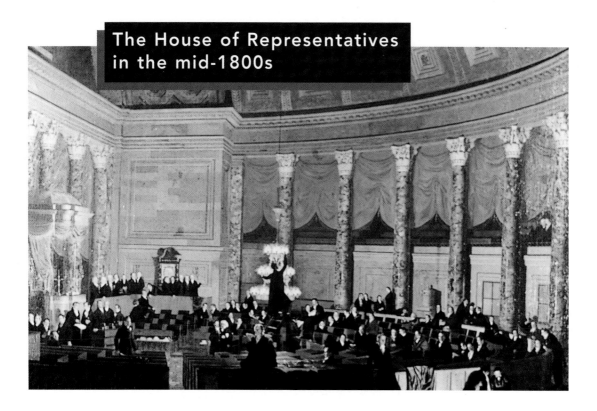

The House of Representatives in the mid-1800s

became known as the Great Compromise.

Because of the Great Compromise, the Constitutional Convention was successful. Our founding fathers wrote an

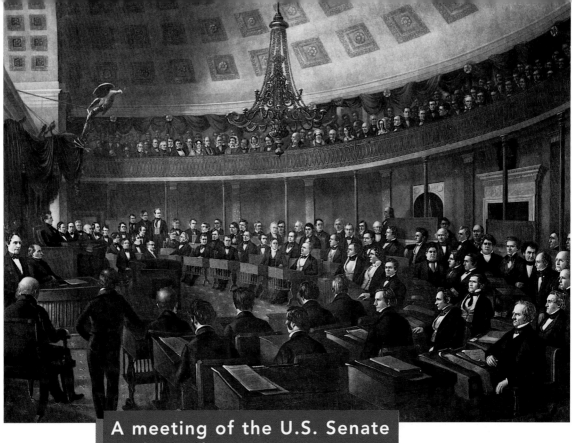

A meeting of the U.S. Senate in the mid-1800s

outstanding plan for government. The United States has used this plan for more than two hundred years.

How Congress Works

Today's Congress is set up much the way its founders planned it. Each state has two senators in the Senate. The number of members sent by each state to the House of Representatives is based on the state's population.

President Bill Clinton addresses a joint session of Congress.

When Congress is not in session, the president can call special sessions of Congress for emergencies. Each house of Congress meets separately in Washington, D.C. However, when there is an important message from the president or a visiting foreign leader, both houses come together in a joint session.

Congress has many jobs. It makes laws that affect everyone living in the United States.

Congress can decide how to tax people and how to use the tax money. Congress makes laws controlling how the United States trades with other countries. Congress also decides whether new states can be admitted to the Union. In 1959, Hawaii became the fiftieth state to be admitted. Presently, Congress is considering whether Puerto Rico should be a state.

Although the president of the United States is the

President Bill Clinton (seated) signs a new bill into law.

commander-in-chief of the armed forces, it is Congress that can declare war against another country.

Every bill passed by Congress has to be shown to the president. The president has ten days to sign the bill and make it a law. The president can also veto a bill, or refuse to approve it. Then that bill will not become a law.

The Supreme Court can undo a law passed by Congress. If judges on the Supreme Court decide that the law goes against the Constitution, they can declare the law to be illegal. Congress may then pass another version of the law or add an amendment, or new rule, to the

Constitution, making it okay to pass the law they want.

Almost all sessions of Congress are open to the public and to reporters. Except for

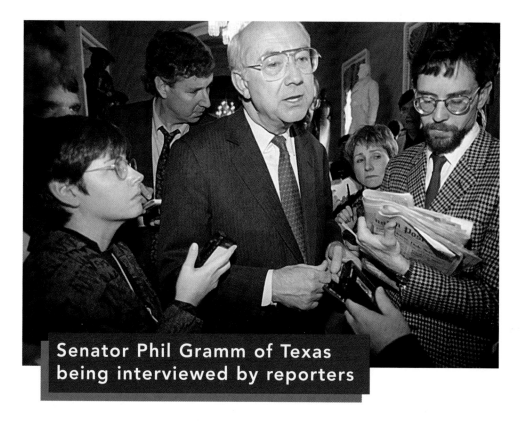

Senator Phil Gramm of Texas being interviewed by reporters

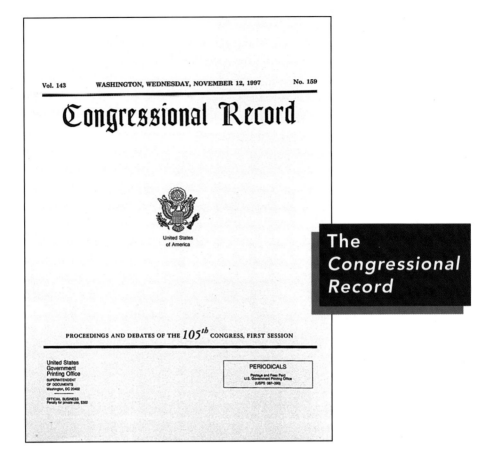

Vol. 143 WASHINGTON, WEDNESDAY, NOVEMBER 12, 1997 No. 159

Congressional Record

United States
of America

PROCEEDINGS AND DEBATES OF THE 105th CONGRESS, FIRST SESSION

United States
Government
Printing Office
SUPERINTENDENT
OF DOCUMENTS
Washington, DC 20402

OFFICIAL BUSINESS
Penalty for private use, $300

PERIODICALS

Postage and Fees Paid
U.S. Government Printing Office
(USPS 087–390)

The
Congressional
Record

some secret military information, everything decided or
discussed by Congress is
published in a report called
the *Congressional Record*.

Both houses of Congress have committees that study problems and new ideas. Some committees are permanent and others are set up to discuss a particular bill.

Committee members research various topics and discuss the details of a possible bill with experts. Once a bill is written, it is then shown to Congress. If it is passed by both houses and signed by the president, it becomes a law.

Senator Thomas Daschle holds up a new bill.

The two largest political parties of the United States, the Democrats and the Republicans, control Congress.

The party with the greatest number of representatives in Congress is known as the majority party. The other party is called the minority party. Members of the majority party are chosen to head the committees. In each house, a majority leader and a minority leader are chosen by their party members. These leaders help schedule and control the discussion of different bills.

The House of Representatives

Today the House of Representatives has 435 members. The states with larger populations have more representatives in the House. The states with smaller populations have fewer. Each state has at least one member.

The government of the United States counts the

people living in the country every ten years. This is called the national census. The census figures tell us how many representatives each state can have in the House.

California has the largest population among the states. Therefore, it has the most representatives—fifty-two. Some states, like Alaska and Vermont, have only one.

The number of members in the House of Representatives is limited to 435. Congress made this law in 1911 so that the House would not get too big.

The representatives are elected to a two-year term by the people in each state. A representative's term in Congress runs from each odd-numbered year to the next odd-numbered year. The representatives then decide if they want to run for office again.

The Constitution says that a representative must be at least twenty-five years old and live in the state where he or she is being elected. Also, a member of the House must have been a citizen of the United States for at least seven years.

The head of the House of Representatives is known as the Speaker of the House.

In 1995, Newt Gingrich became Speaker of the House.

That person is picked by members of the majority party and elected by the House. If both the president and vice president of the United States die or step down from their jobs, the speaker becomes president. The speaker appoints the members of all temporary committees. The speaker can also vote but usually doesn't unless there is a tie.

Our Representatives at Work

Our members of Congress never know where their jobs might take them. One day they may meet in their offices with their new staff. Another day they may be leading a holiday parade or visiting the scene of an emergency in their home state.

Congresswoman Tillie Fowler meets with her staff. Together they work to set up appointments, research bills, and communicate with the public.

Former Speaker of the House "Tip" O'Neill (left) leads a Saint Patrick's Day parade. Senator Sam Nunn (right) visits devasted areas after Hurricane Andrew.

The Senate

The Senate has one hundred members, called senators. Each state has two senators regardless of its population. Since 1913, senators have been elected by the people who live in each state.

A U.S. senator must be at least thirty years old and live

In 1994, Senate candidates Diane Feinstein and Michael Huffington of California debated on *Larry King Live*.

Long-term Senators

There's no limit to the number of terms a senator can serve. These senators have all enjoyed long terms in office. Some are still serving.

Senator Margaret Chase Smith (Republican, Maine) served from 1954 to 1972.

Strom Thurmond (Republican, South Carolina) was first elected to the Senate in 1955.

Senator Edward Kennedy (Democrat, Massachusetts) has been in the Senate since 1962.

in the state he or she serves. A senator must have been a citizen of the United States for at least nine years.

The term of office for a senator is six years, but not all senators' terms end at the same time. Only about thirty-three senators seek re-election at one time.

The members of the Senate vote on people that the president of the United States chooses for certain jobs. For example, when the president chooses a person to serve as a justice on the Supreme Court, the Senate must agree to it by a majority vote. First, a Senate committee interviews and investigates the candidate. The committee then tells the entire Senate whether the candidate should be approved for the Supreme Court. Then, the Senate votes for or against the candidate. If the Senate disapproves of a candidate, then the president must choose another person. This keeps the president from having too much power over choices for the Supreme Court.

Another job the Senate has is to ratify, or accept, treaties that the president makes with other countries. Treaties are agreements. The Senate must approve them by a two-thirds majority. That means at least sixty-seven of the one hundred senators must agree.

Congressional Hearings

Committees in Congress learn more about a possible bill by listening to other Americans. Every year they hold congressional hearings on various subjects. People on different sides of an issue come to express their views.

(Counterclockwise from top) The U.S. Senate hears testimony about soldiers of war still missing in action or taken as prisoners. Whoopi Goldberg testifies before the Senate on how budget cuts will affect the country. Members on this congressional panel discuss healthcare benefits.

Your Opinion Matters!

Perhaps you would like to ask your congressman or congress-woman a question. Perhaps you have something you would like to suggest to him or her. Your opinion matters! Maybe you would like to arrange for a tour of the Capitol. Write your congressperson a letter.

Address it like this:

Congressman(woman) (name)
U.S. House of Representatives
Washington, DC 20515

Senator (name)
U.S. Senate
Washington, DC 20510

Being elected to Congress is an honor. People trust the members of Congress to represent them on important government matters. Every year, seventy-four high school juniors from across the

Every year, seventy-four high school juniors work as Congressional helpers called pages.

country are chosen to work as Congressional helpers called pages. Perhaps someday you will be a page at the United States Congress!

To Find Out More

Here are some additional resources to help you learn more about Congress:

 **Books**

Carter, Alden R. **The American Revolution: War for Independence.** Franklin Watts, 1992.

Feinberg, Barbara Silberdick. **The National Government.** Franklin Watts, 1993.

Quiri, Patricia Ryon. **The Constitution.** Children's Press, 1998.

Quiri, Patricia Ryon. **The Presidency.** Children's Press, 1998.

Weber, Michael. **Our Congress.** Millbrook Press, 1994.

Organizations and Online Sites

E-mail Your Congressperson
http://lcweb.loc.gov/global/ legislative/email.html

Use your zip code to find your congressperson's e-mail address.

Kids Voting
http://www.kidsvoting. interpath.net/resources. html

Devoted to educating young people about voting.

Library of Congress
10 First Street SE
Washington, D.C. 20540
http://kweb.loc.gov/

Contains the entire library of Thomas Jefferson, thousands of government documents, and more. Tours available daily.

National Archives
700 Pennsylvania Ave. NW
Washington, D.C. 20408
http://www.nara.gov/

Original documents of the Constitution and Bill of Rights on view.

National Museum of American History
Smithsonian Institution
Washington, DC 20560
http://www.si.edu/ organiza/museums/nmah/

Exhibitions about early American history.

U.S. House of Representatives
http://www.house.gov/

Everything you need to know about the House and its members.

U.S. Senate
http://www.senate.gov/

Complete information about the Senate and the Capitol.

Important Words

amendment change in the Constitution

bill a proposed law

census a count of the population

citizen person entitled to full legal rights and privileges

compromise an agreement

convention meeting

delegates people who represent states

federal nationwide

independence freedom

majority the larger group

minority the smaller group

population the number of people living in an area

ratify accept

treaty agreement between countries

veto reject

Index

Meet the Author

Patricia Ryon Quiri lives in Palm Harbor, Florida, with her husband Bob and three sons. Ms. Quiri graduated from Alfred University in upstate New York and has a B.A. in elementary education. She currently teaches second grade in the Pinellas County School system. Other books by Ms. Quiri include *The Presidency, The Declaration of Independence, The Constitution, The Supreme Court,* and *The Bill of Rights.* Ms. Quiri has also written a five-book series on American landmarks and symbols for Children's Press.